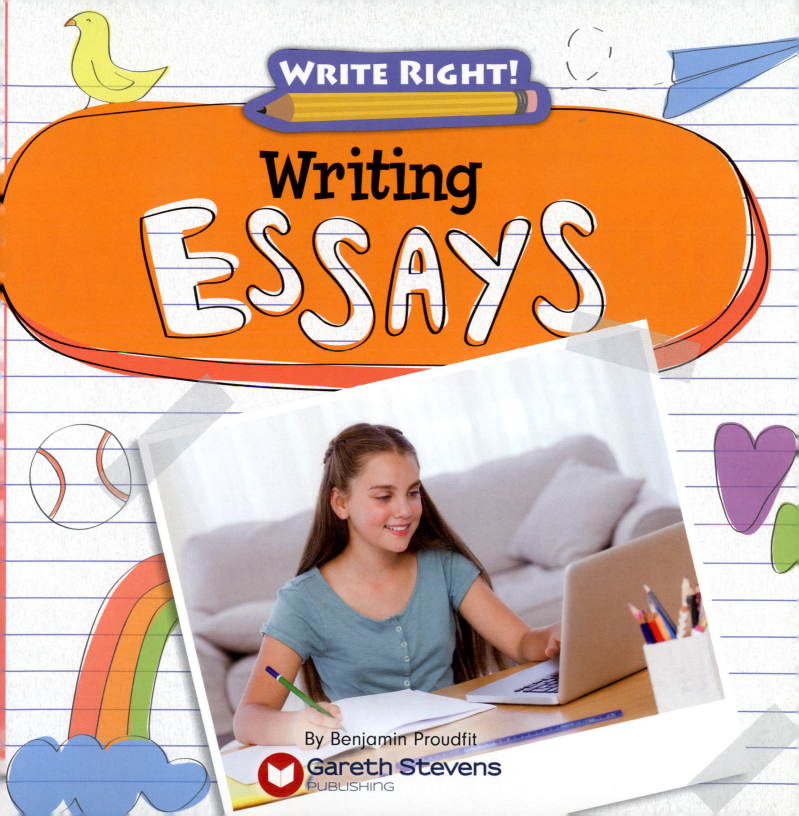

Write Right!

Writing ESSAYS

By Benjamin Proudfit

Gareth Stevens
PUBLISHING

Please visit our website, www.garethstevens.com. For a free color catalog of all our high-quality books, call toll free 1-800-542-2595 or fax 1-877-542-2596.

Library of Congress Cataloging-in-Publication Data

Proudfit, Benjamin.
Writing essays / by Benjamin Proudfit.
p. cm. — (Write right!)
Includes index.
ISBN 978-1-4824-1138-6 (pbk.)
ISBN 978-1-4824-1139-3 (6-pack)
ISBN 978-1-4824-1137-9 (library binding)
1. Report writing — Juvenile literature. 2. Composition (Language arts) — Juvenile literature. 3. Essay — Authorship — Juvenile literature. I. Title.
PE1408.P76 2015
808.042—d23

First Edition

Published in 2015 by
Gareth Stevens Publishing
111 East 14th Street, Suite 349
New York, NY 10003

Copyright © 2015 Gareth Stevens Publishing

Designer: Sarah Liddell
Editor: Kristen Rajczak

Photo credits: Cover, p. 1 wavebreakmedia/Shutterstock.com; p. 5 Tyler Olson/Shutterstock.com; p. 7 (main) bloomua/Shutterstock.com; p. 7 (lined paper) Mega Pixel/Shutterstock.com; p. 9 (main) xalanx/iStock/Thinkstock.com; p. 9 (thought bubble) Stock Montage/Contributor/Archive Photos/Getty Images; p. 11 monkeybusinessimages/iStock/Thinkstock.com; p. 13 michaeljung/Shutterstock.com; p. 15 Top Photo Group/Top Photo Group/Thinkstock.com; p. 17 christingasner/iStock/Thinkstock.com; p. 19 Monkey Business Images/Shutterstock.com; p. 21 (background) mexrix/Shutterstock.com; p. 21 (girl) Asier Romero/Shutterstock.com.

Printed in the United States of America

CPSIA compliance information: Batch #CS15GS: For further information contact Gareth Stevens, New York, New York at 1-800-542-2595.

CONTENTS

Words in the glossary appear in **bold** type the first time they are used in the text.

WHAT IS AN ESSAY?

An essay is a short piece of writing. It may be an **assignment** in your social studies, science, or language arts class. Essay questions are also common on tests. You need knowledge of a topic and good writing skills to write an essay.

Essay assignments can be worded in many ways:

- Write an essay giving three ways Eastern Woodland Indians used nature.

- How did the Eastern Woodland Indians use the world around them? Give three examples.

- Support this idea: Eastern Woodland Indians used their surroundings in their daily lives.

ON THE WRITE TRACK

There are many kinds of essays, including those that compare two topics or ideas. This book will focus mainly on **informative** essays.

The examples on page 4 all ask that you tell how Eastern Woodland Indians used nature. They just do so in different ways.

OUTLINE IT!

Once you have your essay topic or question, read it closely. Make sure you understand what you are being asked to do in the essay. Are you asked for examples or **details**? How many should you give?

The first step of a good essay is an outline. It's the road map of your essay and lists what it will include. You don't have to write in complete sentences. Just use words or **phrases** that will remind you of what you want to write and the order it will be in.

ON THE WRITE TRACK

At times, an outline will be part of your essay writing assignment. Be sure to follow your teacher's directions when making an outline that's part of your grade.

As this sample outline shows, outlines help you plan your writing. The following sections in the book will explain the parts of an essay included here.

Essay Question:

How did Eastern Woodland Indians use the world around them? Give three examples.

Topic sentence: Eastern Woodland Indians used their surroundings

Example 1: built homes out of trees

Example 2: traveled on rivers and lakes

Example 3: hunted and fished for food

Conclusion: many ways of using area and animals around them

WRITING A TOPIC SENTENCE

An essay begins with a topic sentence. It's a statement that answers a question or introduces your topic.

One simple way to write a topic sentence is to restate the question you've been asked.

Question: How did Eastern Woodland Indians use the world around them?

Topic sentence: Eastern Woodland Indians used the world around them in many ways.

Then, try to make the sentence more **specific** and interesting. Here's the example above rewritten:

The Eastern Woodland Indians found many ways to use the **natural resources** in their surroundings.

ON THE WRITE TRACK

Your topic sentence should start with a capital letter and end with a period, since it's a statement. It should have a **subject** and **verb** to be a complete sentence.

SHOW YOUR SUPPORT

Now you're ready to support your topic sentence. "Support" means "to hold up" or "help." So, each of the examples or details you write in your essay should "hold up" what you've stated in your topic sentence.

Look back at your outline. Write a complete sentence or two to explain each of the points you listed there. One detail in an assignment about the Eastern Woodland Indians is written below:

The Eastern Woodland Indians lived near forests. They used the trees' wood to build their homes.

ON THE WRITE TRACK

When moving between examples, use transition words such as "also," "another," and "in addition." These words show how the ideas connect to one another.

The part of your essay that includes examples or details is often called the "body" of the essay.

11

FINDING DETAILS

Essay assignments are often about topics you're learning about in class. Support for your topic sentence may be right in your textbook.

Other times, you'll need to find examples and details. You can go to the library and find a few books about the topic. The Internet is another source of information. However, make sure the websites you visit are trustworthy. They should have an address that ends in .gov or .edu, or be connected with a known organization, such as the National Geographic Society.

ON THE WRITE TRACK

Anyone can make a website and write whatever they want on it. That's why you need to be careful about where your information comes from.

IN CONCLUSION...

The conclusion is the ending sentence that sums up the rest of your essay. Transition words and phrases are an important part of the conclusion. You want to let the reader know the essay is nearing its end! Use "finally," "in conclusion," "as the examples show," or other words of summary or conclusion.

Here's a sample conclusion for the essay about the Eastern Woodland Indians:

In summary, the surroundings of the Eastern Woodland Indians greatly affected how they ate, moved, and lived.

ON THE WRITE TRACK

Sometimes your teacher will tell you to include your opinion in the conclusion.

The conclusion example on page 14 shows how the topic sentence and examples work together.

The Eastern Woodland Indians

The Eastern Woodland Indians found many ways to use the natural resources in their surroundings. This group of Indians hunted animals in their region to [...] They also used the bones of animals to make tools [and] weapons. To travel, the Eastern Woodland Ind[ians] built simple boats and canoes to navigate the la[kes and] rivers near their homes. The Eastern Woodland Ind[ians] lived near forests, too. They used the trees' wood to bu[ild] their homes. In summary, the surroundings of the Eastern Woodland Indians greatly affected how they ate, moved, and lived.

REVISING

Have you finished writing your essay? You're not done yet. It's time to read through your sentences to see if anything needs to be revised, or changed. Ask yourself these questions while revising:

- Did I answer the question in my assignment?
- Do I have all the parts needed in an essay, including a topic sentence, supporting sentences, and a conclusion?
- Is everything spelled correctly?
- Are all my sentences complete with capital letters, punctuation marks, subjects, and verbs?
- Is my handwriting neat enough to read?

ON THE WRITE TRACK

The first try at a piece of writing is often called a "rough draft."

When you read over your essay, see if you can improve any of the sentences. Make them clearer, use more specific words, or take out unnecessary words.

TEST QUESTIONS

Does your test include an essay question? Don't worry! The writing process doesn't change. Use scrap paper to write a quick outline of your answer. Be sure to start your answer with a topic sentence that directly answers the question. Follow the sentence with supporting details and a short conclusion.

Often, teachers will tell you what the essay questions on a test may be. In that case, write an outline for each possible question ahead of time. You'll be prepared for anything!

ON THE WRITE TRACK

Don't skip the outlining step of writing your essay to save time while taking a test. It helps you fully answer the question and plan the order of your information, making your final essay better.

Essay questions test your knowledge as well as your writing skills. Paying attention in class and studying for the test will help you with the content of the essay.

19

MORE PARAGRAPHS?

A longer essay follows a similar structure to a short essay, but it has a **paragraph** for each part, not just a sentence or two. It becomes even more important to outline your essay when you have many paragraphs to organize.

Longer essays start with an introduction, which includes a main topic sentence that tells what the essay will be about as a whole. The body of the essay includes paragraphs explaining each supporting idea. The last paragraph is your conclusion.

ON THE WRITE TRACK

Each paragraph of an essay should have its own topic sentence and only cover one idea.

SAMPLE SHORT ESSAY

Assignment: Write an essay including three examples of how writing is used in daily life.

Writing is a part of everyone's daily life. Students write to show their knowledge on tests and in essays. People communicate by writing e-mails and text messages, too. In addition, news reporters and authors write so people can get information. In conclusion, writing is a way people communicate every day.

- topic sentence
- example 1
- example 2
- example 3
- conclusion

GLOSSARY

assignment: a task or amount of work given to do

communicate: to share thoughts or feelings by sound, movement, or writing

detail: a small part

informative: having to do with knowledge obtained from study or observation

natural resource: something in nature that can be used by people

paragraph: a group of sentences having to do with one idea or topic

phrase: a group of words

specific: clearly stated

subject: the person, place, or thing that does the main action of the sentence

verb: action word

vocabulary: the words someone knows

FOR MORE INFORMATION

BOOKS

Minden, Cecilia, and Kate Roth. *How to Write an Essay*. Ann Arbor, MI: Cherry Lake Publishing, 2013.

Willis, Meredith Sue. *Blazing Pencils: Writing Stories and Essays*. Millburn, NJ: Montemayor Press, 2013.

WEBSITES

Binky's Facts and Opinions
pbskids.org/arthur/games/factsopinions/factsopinions.html
Play this game to practice deciding if a statement is a fact or an opinion.

Homework Helper
www.timeforkids.com/homework-helper/a-plus-papers
Find tips about writing many kinds of essays as well as book reports, biographies, and more.

INDEX